SHORT ·
NID

PAUL HANNON

HILLSIDE PUBLICATIONS

20 Wheathead Crescent
Keighley
West Yorkshire
BD22 6LX

First Published 2009

© Paul Hannon 2009

ISBN 978 1 870141 90 1

*The sketch maps are based on 1947 OS one-inch maps
and earlier OS six-inch maps*

Cover illustration: Brimham Rocks
Back cover: Springtime at Ramsgill
Page 1: Yorke's Folly, Guise Cliff
(Paul Hannon/Hillslides Picture Library)

Printed by Steffprint
Unit 5, Keighley Industrial Park
Royd Ings Avenue
Keighley
West Yorkshire
BD21 4DZ

CONTENTS

INTRODUCTION

Nidderdale is probably least known of the major valleys of the Yorkshire Dales, as neighbouring Wharfedale and Wensleydale siphon off visitors to leave Nidderdale free from congestion. Virtually all this guide falls within the Nidderdale Area of Outstanding Natural Beauty, designated in 1994, belatedly so for a landscape of such quality.

Nidderdale proper divides into two distinct halves. Above Pateley Bridge is a well-defined upper Dales valley, increasingly steep flanks rising above the narrow dale floor to moorland heights. Sleepy villages and sheep farms straggle out towards reservoirs that occupy a bleak setting in a bowl of high fells. Other features of the upper dale include Goyden Pot, How Stean Gorge and Gouthwaite Reservoir, while the settlements of Ramsgill, Middlesmoor, Lofthouse and Wath share a timeless quality. Downstream from Pateley Bridge the Nidd Valley is far more pastoral, sweeping gracefully through a landscape of fields and woodland. Even below Pateley there remain glorious pockets of moorland, most famously at Brimham Rocks and Guise Cliff, the most colourful corner of all Nidderdale.

This dark gritstone landscape is evident in the aforementioned locations, though it is the less common appearance of limestone on the floor of the upper dale that provides the delights of the How Stean Gorge area. Aside from natural rockscapes and man-made lakes Nidderdale boasts two other outstanding aspects - heather and trees. The valley is lavished with attractive woodland, while the heather moors reach endlessly over sweeping horizons. Before passing to the abbeys of Fountains and Byland, Nidderdale was a Royal hunting chase, and today much of this vast moorland is managed as grouse shooting country.

Many of the walks can be accessed by bus, the main service from Harrogate linking Pateley Bridge with a seasonal service higher up the dale. Whilst the route description should be sufficient to guide you around each walk, a map is recommended for greater information: Ordnance Survey 1:25,000 scale maps give the finest detail, and Explorer 298 covers virtually all of the walks.

Packhorse bridge, Thornthwaite

USEFUL INFORMATION

·Nidderdale AONB
Council Offices, King Street, Pateley Bridge HG3 5LE
(01423-712950)
·Pateley Bridge Tourist Information (01423-711147)
·Harrogate Tourist Information (01423-537300)
·Yorkshire Dales Society (01729-825600)
(working to protect the area's natural beauty)
·The National Trust Regional Office (01904-702021)
·Ramblers' Association
2nd Floor, Camelford House, 87-89 Albert Embankment,
London SE1 7BR (020-7339 8500)
·Open Access (0845-100 3298) www.countrysideaccess.gov.uk
·Traveline - public transport information (0870-608260)

NIDDERDALE

20 Short Scenic Walks

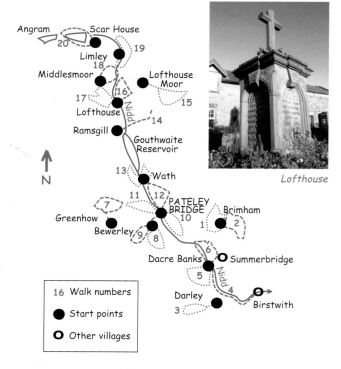

Angram
Scar House
20
19
Limley
18
Middlesmoor
17
16
Lofthouse
Moor
15
Lofthouse
14
Ramsgill
Gouthwaite
Reservoir
13
Wath
11 12
PATELEY
BRIDGE
7
Brimham
Greenhow
10
1
2
Bewerley
9 8
6
Dacre Banks
Summerbridge
5
Darley
4
3
Birstwith

Nidd

Nidd

↑
N

Lofthouse

16	Walk numbers
●	Start points
O	Other villages

6

A RECORD OF YOUR WALKS

WALK	DATE	NOTES
1		
2		
3		
4		
5		
6		
7		
8		
9		
10		
11		
12		
13		
14		
15		
16		
17		
18		
19		
20		

4³4 miles
from Brimham Rocks

A beautifully wooded side valley plays support to the weirdly sculpted celebrity rocks

Start Brimham Rocks (GR: 208645), National Trust car park
Map OS Explorer 298, Nidderdale

Brimham Rocks form an extensive collection of millstone grit outcrops, sculpted into wonderfully bizarre shapes by millions of years of Yorkshire weather. Scattered about the moor they form the ultimate natural playground for playful children and serious rock climbers. From the car park a broad way leads directly to Brimham House, saving the intervening attractions for journey's end. Built in 1792 for Lord Grantley's keeper, it serves as a shop and information point: refreshments and WCs are on hand. Take the main path left of the house: further splendid outcrops include the Dancing Bear and Idol Rock. Beyond the last rocks the firm path loops back right: leave it by a green path which maintains a northerly aim above the wood. Further, it drops down onto a farm drive. Double back left on this through woods to approach Brimham Rocks Farm (High North Pasture on maps). Before it, however, leave at the first gate on the right after the trees. Cross the field to a gate at the end, and on to a small gate in the far right corner in front of North Pasture Farm. Enter the yard by another such gate, and leave by one on the left after the main buildings.

Bear right across the field, dropping slightly to a gate in a fence by a tiny stream. Continue straight on a more open field to a gate at the head of a walled green way. Turn down its pleasant course as it drops to cross Fell Beck to a clutch of houses. After one on the left, pass through the yard to a stile, then cross to a small bridge with a gate behind. Turn right down the field outside the stream to a stile into trees in the corner. A path slants left up the wooded bank to a fence at the top, going right with it past modest Knoxstone Crags. Keep on with the fence to drop back into trees. The clear path runs pleasantly on to reach a stile into a big field (woodland on the map!). Turn right down an inviting track to the bottom corner, with a stile, footbridge and cobbled ford. Don't cross but bear left on a path gradually rising through the trees.

Approaching a walled enclosure the path forks: keep right, on the level through hollies to leave the trees at a stile below Low Wood's isolated buildings. A path crosses to join a wider one descending from the left. Remain level to enter birchwoods, later merging into a broader path from the right. Go left a short way to arrive beneath ruinous buildings, where the path doubles back down to the right. From a footbridge on Fell Beck a path runs downstream, partly on the bank of a mill-race. Further, with a millpond to the left, pass beneath a massive wall to emerge onto the road through Smelthouses, a charming hamlet in a setting to match. A rich assortment of dwellings stand near the beck, where lead ore was brought for smelting by the monks of Fountains Abbey. Difficult to imagine this sequestered spot as a hive of activity! Turn left over the bridge and a short way up the road to a drive on the left at Wysing House. Just past the attractive buildings at Low Wood House the track swings left. Here leave it by a gate on the right to follow a superb walled track, rising ever steadily through greenery.

Beyond the walls this Monks' Trod rises by a wood, then into more open surrounds: High Wood comes up and the path leaves the trees, outcrops now dominant on the left. Through a gate at the top you emerge onto the moor road. Heading left onto Brimham Moor, the drive to the car park leaves the road to finish the walk, though an earlier fork sees a branch remain on the moor to escape the road earlier. Time to go exploring again!

Dancing Bear, Brimham Rocks

9

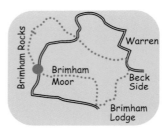

*4¾ miles
from Brimham Rocks*

**Easy walking
through a peaceful,
colourful and
unsung landscape**

*Start Brimham Rocks (GR: 208645), National Trust car park
Map OS Explorer 298, Nidderdale*

From the car park return to the road crossing Brimham
Moor. Go right for 100 yards and turn off left on an inviting path
through rolling heather. Though of modest extent, this National
Trust land appears greater as it sweeps away to the left. Further
back, some of the celebrated rocks rise from the bracken and
woodland surrounds. At the end a gate in a boundary wall sees you
off the moor, and a nice path heads away through still colourful
terrain. This emerges onto a farm drive beneath Riva Hill, and runs
to a corner. Here leave the farm road which swings left, and take
a gate to the right, where a green track heads away. This runs a
lengthy enclosed way as a cart track to ultimately emerge onto a road.

Ignoring the road take a farm road left to Brimham Lodge.
Look right to see the remarkable facade of this lovely house, dating from the 1660s and boasting an astonishing array of mullioned
windows. Outside its garden wall a mounting block supports a stone
shaft into which is set an old sundial. Remain on the access road
left of the house, through the yard and down the slope beyond.
This same track continues past a wood and on to the farm at Park
House. Pass right of the buildings along another walled green track.
At the end ignore the gate in front and take one to the right. Head
away along the wallside to a gate at the end, where an enclosed
path swings left above a string of wildfowl ponds. Remain on the
path to Beck Side Farm, and out on its drive onto a narrow lane.

Turn right past an old chapel to a junction, then left on South Lane. Passing South Farm take a stile on the left, on a slight brow. Head away with the wall, and a fence takes over then turns left towards South Farm. Don't follow it but keep straight on, crossing to the left side of the re-forming wall to drop to a wood. Enter at a wall-gap at a recessed corner and drop to a little beck. Across, bear left, rising away and on between beck and fence to meet a broad path rising through trees. Turn up to a gate out of the wood, and a faint green way traces a line of trees to Summer Wood House. Head up the drive onto Brimham Moor to meet the road. Cross to a little path rising through bracken to large outcrops above. Behind, a thin path rises through heather into bracken, running a level course left to meet a better path. Double back right up this, rising steadily left onto the moortop and striding north-west to the first outcrop: in front of it it swings left to cross to a cluster of rocks dominated by a shapely, top-heavy specimen. From here the best route is to drop down the heathery bank to an access road below.

Turn left along the edge of the moor for only a minute or so before a good path slants back up onto the moor, opposite a gate. With boulders above, it rises above the trees and runs for some while in a groove to meet a broad, solid path. The right option runs past myriad outcrops to soon reach Brimham House. Conclude on the main path heading directly away, with options to branch off on any number of offshoots before emerging back at the car park.

Brimham Rocks

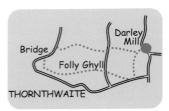

3¹₂ miles
from Darley

An absorbing exploration
of a peaceful and
colourful side valley

Start Darley Head (GR: 193598), lay-by opposite Darley Mill
Map OS Explorer 298, Nidderdale (or 297)

Dating from the 17th century, imposing Darley Mill is now a popular retail venue with cafe. Go left past the mill, and after the house above, take a stile on the right. Darley's pub, the Wellington, is a minute further. Head along the fieldside, through a couple of stiles. Ignoring a footbridge on Darley Beck, bear left across the field to a corner stile above a bend of the beck. A short enclosed path rises above the beck to end at a stile, where rise up the field, briefly. Go right to a stile in a recess, then slant up to find a stile opposite, at the top of a hedge. Slant again to a stile in the top wall just short of a gate, then up the wallside to a stile onto a road.

Turn right past two fine houses with views over this well wooded valley. Before a group of houses take a stile to descend the wallside to another. Go left with the hedge atop unkempt pasture before delving into scrub. A stone causey features amid the dense undergrowth by the beck. At the end is a gate onto a road at Folly Gill Bridge in front of Thornthwaite Mill. Cross onto the drive between the main buildings, emerging into a field. This cart track crosses to shadow the beck, rising to become enclosed to reach the former Folly Ghyll Mill, a remarkable surprise tucked away here. Continue up the access road past the large house Folly Ghyll, as far as a sharp bend. Take a stile in front and ascend the field outside a wood to scattered trees and rocks at the top. An imposing wall-stile leads onto a drive. Go just a few yards right to a stile hidden behind a holly, and a good path rises through birch, bracken and boulders. Towards the top keep right to a corner stile onto a drive.

Go right, briefly, but as it turns down to a house take a stile on the left. Cross a field bottom to the next stile, then over a drive to a stile ahead, above another house. A briefly enclosed path resumes before emerging into a field to maintain this line. The 'stile of the day' is encountered, with stone kerbing in evidence. At a drive, cross straight over and across one last field to a stile onto another drive. Turn down into the yard of the second house, where a small gate to its right accesses the head of an enclosed path. This descends with a stream to emerge onto Church Lane. Turn down to St Saviour's church, Thornthwaite: stained glass features heroines Florence Nightingale and Grace Darling. Resume down the road to a stile accessing a gem of a tiny packhorse bridge (see page 5), in a peaceful wooded setting on a monastic route to Fountains Abbey.

Back on the road, ascend to the drive along to Carr Lodge Farm. Turn up briefly after barns on the left and slant right up to a stile onto a track. Cross to a stile and slant to a wall-stile on the right just short of the field corner. Entering trees, go briefly left along the edge then the path turns to cross this slender belt to a stile back out. Ahead are big Nidd Valley views from Brimham Rocks to Darley. Head straight down to a gate below, from where a grassy wallside track runs out onto a road opposite Oxen Close Farm. Go left for two minutes to a stile on the right. Head down the field to a stile in the wall, then down two fieldsides to one in the corner. Head away with Darley Beck, and when a low wall begins cross it and go the few yards further to a stile leading to a footbridge on the beck. Across it you rejoin the outward route to finish.

Folly Ghyll Mill

*4¾ miles
from Dacre Banks*

**A delightful linear walk
tracing the Nidderdale Way
down the lower valley
between lovely villages**

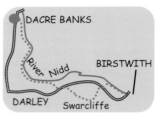

Start Village centre (GR: 196619), car park by pub
Finish Birstwith, return by bus (regular service)
Map OS Explorer 298, Nidderdale

From the green take the little lane between pub and car park, and quickly branch left down into a yard. Drop down and along to the right near more houses, and at the end take a gate on the left. Pass through a gate then cross to one ahead. From here a thin path crosses to the riverbank: turn right for an extended ramble by the Nidd. The path encounters the former railway alongside an underpass: with the embankment on the right the path soon enjoys greater freedom as it ambles on to a footbridge on Darley Beck. The linear village of Darley is seen up to the right. The path runs along the garden foots of prestige dwellings on the site of Darley's station: a final open section leads to a footbridge on the river.

Ignoring this, turn right to join a broader track - the old railway. At this path crossroads turn left, parallel with the river on a track over a farm bridge on a stream. Across, rise into the field above and follow the top of a wooded bank, a pleasant course between holly and brambles to emerge at a stile into a field. Head diagonally across a couple of fields to the houses at The Holme, where a stile admits onto the road. Turn left on the footway past these scattered dwellings, noting thatched Holme Hall on the right.

After the last house take a stile on the right and cross to the far corner of the field. Head away with a wall, and at the trees at the end, rise a few yards before crossing a couple more pastures parallel with the road below. A stile gives access to a woodland corner, and a path runs through bracken to a rising bridlepath. Turn up into the wood of Reynard Crag, this substantially flagged old way climbing through rich birchwood. Beyond a gate at the top it continues in delightful fashion up the side of the wood to emerge onto a lane end at Swarcliffe. Continue a little further to Rennie Crag Farm, then turn left along a drive. This vantage point has extensive views updale, over a great curve of the valley to the high moors; Brimham Rocks are also prominent across the dale.

By the house at the bottom go straight down a path into trees, a super woodside descent with fine views over the Birstwith neighbourhood. Towards the bottom descend a fieldside onto the valley road. Turn right for a short while, a gentle rise with a decent verge. At a bend escape left down a narrow lane by Birstwith House. With a farm on the right, note the house of 1688 with mullioned windows on the left. From a gate at the bottom a track continues down, and a path takes over to approach the river. Though the route takes a stile on the right, advance a few yards further to admire the beautiful arch of New Bridge. On a Skipton-Ripon pack-horse route and dating from around 1615, it was rebuilt in 1822.

Back at the stile commence a lovely section downstream, soon cutting out a river bend to shadow a hedge. Ahead is Birstwith feeds mill, while over to the right is the rather more elegant spire of St James' church. At the end the river is rejoined to enter Birstwith: a mill-race shadowing the route out to the road from its weir on the Nidd. Just to the left the river bridge leads to the Old Station Inn, to the right is the shop - and bus stop.

Rambling by the Nidd below Dacre Banks

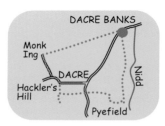

*3¾ miles
from Dacre Banks*

**Richly varied attractions
are found on this easy
walk around the hilltop
hamlet of Dacre**

*Start Village centre (GR: 196619), car park by pub
Map OS Explorer 298, Nidderdale*

Dacre Banks is a pleasant village with name and setting to match. It has a pub, the Royal Oak, shop and WC: Holy Trinity church stands near to the river. From the green take the lane between the pub and the car park. When it swings left at the end, keep straight on an enclosed path to a stile into the field ahead. Head away, bearing right to merge with the old railway. Opened in 1862 largely to serve industry in the dale, it ran to Pateley Bridge from near Harrogate and finally closed in 1964. By the far end you fully join the line, passing through a kissing-gate to trace the trackbed. Remain on this for a good while, passing through the farm at Low Hall. There is a glimpse of the old house down to the left, its triple gabled frontage featuring mullioned and transomed windows. Beyond here the track heads on through Low Hall Wood.

At the other end advance just as far as the next gate, through which turn right along the wallside. Passing through a gateway you meet the farthest point of the wood, and here turn left along the wallside. Reaching Pyefield farm road at the end, turn right along it to climb through the fields to Dacre, entering alongside a cluster of buildings at the imposing Dacre Hall. This pleasing hilltop hamlet features a Providence Chapel of 1827 and a WC.

Cross to a lovely cottage, and just to its left take a short drive. At the rear of the houses advance slightly right to a small gate, and a path runs through a small allotment to a stile hidden in the corner. Ascend the fieldsides to a wall-stile at the top onto a

16

drive between houses at Sand House Farm on Hackler's Hill. Rise and cross a cattle-grid to the right, but before following the drive out, take a short detour to the Quaker burial ground. From the grid double back left above the fence to a kissing-gate in the corner. A panel provides more detail of the burial ground, located down the wallside ahead: a door beneath a 1682 datestone gives access. The Society of Friends used this walled enclosure from 1688 to 1842, and a row of gravestones stands beneath the bottom wall.

Back on the drive, it quickly runs out above the farm onto a road. Turn uphill, levelling out to a junction. Go right on Lane Foot Road to a junction with Monk Ing Road. Turn right, ignoring the first drive left. On the skyline ahead are Brimham Rocks. Continue down to a cattle-grid and stile at the bottom. As the farm road turns left to Eastwoods, take a stile on the right and slant down the reedy field to a wall-stile in the bottom corner, then go right to a fence-stile. Curve round the corner and descend with a wall on your right. From a gate at the bottom corner a track winds down to Hill Top Farm. Pass straight through and down its access track. As it swings to the right, now level, look for a kissing-gate on the left. Descend successive wallsides to an unlikely gate in the corner, which admits to the top of an old farmyard. Drop straight down again, and down the access road, Grange Lane, which quickly swings left. Just along to the right is the site of the railway station. At this bend go straight down a pathway in front to join suburban Grange Road to re-enter the village.

Cottage at Dacre

*4¹2 miles
from Dacre Banks*

**Lovely woodland
and riverside
scenery either side
of Low Laithe**

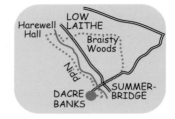

*Start Village centre (GR: 196619), car park by pub
Map OS Explorer 298, Nidderdale*

From the green take the short lane past the Royal Oak,
and quickly branch left down into a yard. Drop down and along to
the right near more houses, and at the end take a gate on the left
by an outhouse. Through a gate cross to a gate ahead from where
a thin path crosses to the river. Turn left to trace the Nidd
upstream to the bridge. Cross to the large sawmill, and an enclosed
path is ushered round the perimeter. At the far end the river is
joined at a weir. Ignore a stile in the fence for a splendid path
upstream. Faced with a wooded bank at the end, the way is ushered
left over a stile and across to a wall-stile onto a rough road. Turn
right, crossing the old railway. Remain on the road, keeping right at
an early fork. The railway soon runs parallel to a gate at the far end.

Passing a lone house, a nicer green track runs alongside a
plantation. From a gate at the end advance along the hedgeside,
and through a gate at the end a track runs to Harewell Hall Farm.
The old house with its mullioned windows is well seen just below:
high above is the Brimham Rocks skyline across the dale. Joining its
access road at the end, drop down and head down into the yard
behind the main house. Opposite the door take a gate on the left
and a grassy track slants down to the old railway, over which head
straight across to a footbridge on the tree-lined riverbank.

Cross and turn downstream, this delightful stretch ends
when deflected left with inflowing Fell Beck. This is crossed by a
footbridge, and from a stile just upstream the path rises up a field

to the road in Low Laithe. Turn right on the footway into the village centre. This small settlement strung along the valley road has a pub, Ye Olde Oak Inn, and a legacy of 19th century textile mills and housing. Past the pub cross to the other side, and immediately after the bus shelter turn up a short driveway. A path continues up the side of a wood, by abundant hollies past a recolonised quarry.

At the top ignore a stile on the left and pass through one at the very top. Just above, turn left on a track towards Braisty Woods hamlet. It passes through a gate and a belt of trees to a junction in the hamlet, where turn right on the access road. A fine big mullioned windowed house stands on the left, with attractive cottages alongside. Advance on past all the buildings and a pond to a fork, where the road goes left. Here go right on an access road to Owenwell House. A charming grassy cart track continues along the base of the woods to end at isolated Woolwich Farm.

Keep on between old walls, through a couple of gates and past a barn to the return of the wood. Through a gate into the trees, a super path runs on the wood edge. Beyond a wall-stile it heads into the centre of Old Spring Wood, a magnificent ancient woodland with hollies in profusion. At the end the path emerges by a lone house. Keep on below it and its drive runs out onto the road at Hartwith Bank. Turn down to the main road in Summerbridge. Here are the Flying Dutchman pub, a Post office, shop, tearoom and chip-shop. Cross straight over and down Dawson Bank to cross the bridge on the Nidd, remaining on the road into Dacre Banks.

Braisty Woods

*3³⁄₄ miles
from Greenhow*

**Outstanding remains of
a fascinating industry
that dominated the
area not that long ago**

*Start Toft Gate, a mile east of village on B6265
Pateley Bridge road (GR: 128643), car park
Map OS Explorer 298, Nidderdale*

A novel feature of this walk is that its highest point is the start. Nearby Greenhow is a remote former lead mining community, its Miners Arms being one of England's highest pubs. Toft Gate is base for an industrial heritage trail. The site can be explored by a path accessing the remains of a square chimney at the top of the flue. A continuation path then runs down to the principal feature, a massive vertical kiln dating from the 1860s.

Start by crossing the main road to the left-hand gate opposite, immediately enjoying extensive views to moors above Upper Nidderdale. A grassy way slants down to a gate then down again, left of a barn to trace the wall to a corner stile. A trod runs to an access road just ahead. Turn right down this to houses at Coldstonesfold, continuing down a grassy track that runs on to join a drive beneath Ivin Waite. Turn down its enclosed course to drop to a junction with a surfaced access road. Double back acutely left on this to its imminent split at Low Hole Bottom. Bear right, rising past the house at Hillend and then running a super course, opening out in more colourful surrounds to reach Brandstone Dub Bridge.

Across, the track climbs by a small wood, levelling out to be joined by one from the right. Keep on the moorland flank of Nabs to a junction. The walk resumes here after a detour to look down on Merryfield mining site. Advance straight on to a gateway, and a little further along you reach a good vantage point above spoil heaps overlooking the mines. The Prosperous Smelt Mill is a large ruinous building by the beck, with a geared winding shaft in situ, and a peat store to its right and the prominent line of an old flue.

For the onward route return to the junction and pass through the gate on the main track. Ignoring a right fork, remain on this walled way as it rises away. At a T-junction above an isolated house turn right, up to bend left to a gate accessing the valley of Brandstone Beck, the environs of Cockhill Lead Mine. The track declines into the gill to enter the old site. On your right is an arch of Providence smelt mill. The track then fords the beck and rises to a junction. Though the route departs left, first advance right to see more of the site. On the flat dale floor are ruins of another smelt mill on the left, with its peat store to the right. A distinctive mine level is sited directly under the track close to the junction.

The onward route cuts sharply left, roughly surfaced and rising gently away. Looking back, a smelt mill chimney appears on the moor above the workings. The way crosses to a wall corner by sheep pens, a little beyond which it ascends to a corner gate. A walled road climbs away, absorbing a farm drive before levelling out. At a sharp right bend just ahead, take a gate on the left and use the Coldstonesfold road declining gently away. It drops more firmly left through open pasture to approach a bend at the bottom. Here rejoin the outward route by taking the thin trod right.

Prosperous Smelt Mill, Merryfield Mines

*4 miles
from Bewerley*

**A stunning combination of
scenery from woodland to
moorland, and a classic
Nidderdale landmark**

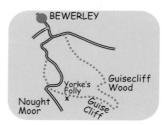

*Start Village centre (GR: 157648), roadside parking
Map OS Explorer 298, Nidderdale*

Bewerley is an attractive village with cottages set back
from a triangular green. Leave by heading south on the footway
through the village. On the left is lovely Bewerley Grange Chapel, a
grange of Fountains Abbey. Continuing, drop past a junction to a T-
junction across Turner Bridge. Go briefly left to take a grassy way
leaving a gate on the right. Running between horse paddocks it
passes through a gate at the end into a field. This faint way runs
on a couple of fieldsides to a corner gate. Resume on the other side
of the hedge, passing a house before a track forms to approach
Baylis Gap Farm. At a muddy corner go forward onto a firm track.

With the farm to the left keep on the track rising away.
At the top it runs on to emerge into a field. Here it turns sharp
right, but keep straight on the wallside ahead to a gate at the end
into Guisecliff Wood. Squeezing through hollies a superb path
heads away, gently rising through this enchanting, boulder-strewn
woodland. At a fork ignore the thinner path ahead and remain on
this broad one swinging sharply uphill. After a short pull it slants
up to the left, but a short detour on a thinner one rising right earns
a near immediate reward as it arrives by the shore of Guisecliff
Tarn. Secreted in deep woodland this proves an unexpected gem!

Leave by going left a few yards along the water's edge
and a path rises away, soon broadening; this rapidly rejoins the
main path to resume through the wood. A delightful, undulating
section runs on to ultimately leave the trees. As a green way it

slants up through bracken to a wall: turn to ascend with it, easing out to approach the top corner by a mast. Big views include skyline features Brimham Rocks and man's 'landmarks' of Knabs Ridge wind turbines and Menwith Hill golf balls. Through a gate onto Heyshaw Moor advance only to the mast's fence corner, then go right with it to cut back to the old wall heading away. After a fence-stile, cross the wall to gain the exposed beginnings of Guise Cliff. Beyond the imposing rock architecture overlooking the woodland blanket below is a wonderful Nidderdale panorama, with Gouthwaite Reservoir up-dale. The path runs left on the crest, with tempting branches seeking out exposed situations: the edge harbours mischievous crevices!

As the edge abates the path runs to a stile where the parallel fence meets a wall. The wallside path continues on the moor edge to the waiting towers of Yorke's Folly, gained by a ladder-stile. This major Nidderdale landmark was built 200 years ago by the Yorkes: one of three original towers succumbed to a storm in 1893. Beyond, the path descends through heather to the road on Nought Bank. From the gate behind follow the main path down the moor. Through a kissing-gate it winds down into the top of Skrikes Wood. The path descends to a stile out of the wood and slants down a large field to a stile back onto the road. Go left down this and along to the junction at Turner Bridge, retracing steps to finish.

Guisecliff Tarn

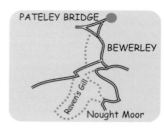

*4¹4 miles
from Pateley Bridge*

**Absorbing woodland,
moorland and gill scenery
above the lovely
village of Bewerley**

*Start Town centre (GR: 157655), car parks
Map OS Explorer 298, Nidderdale*

Cross the bridge at the foot of the High Street and along the road to the edge of town, Bridgehouse Gate, where a side road goes left to Bewerley: double back right at the first junction on a road climbing out. After a couple of minutes take a stile on the left and head directly up the field, through a collapsed wall to the top. Deflecting right to a gap-stile, descend a wallside to a kissing-gate into Fishpond Wood. Take the main path into the heart of the wood with a tiny stream, which you cross by a footbridge before reaching the shore of the rather overgrown yet attractive ornamental lake.

Towards the end of the bank a broader path is met, turn right to swing round to a stile alongside a narrow road. Joining a drive drop down onto the road itself. Turn right, crossing Raven's Gill then spiralling steeply uphill. As Skrikes Wood ends on the left, take a gate and ascend steeply through bracken up the wallside outside trees, with an old sunken way materialising to your right. After a stiff pull a gap in a cross-wall is reached: the true path is fifty yards to the right, where the old track rises to a stile hidden by bracken. Now in a field, slant right up to an outer wall corner, and up two fieldsides to a stile onto a farm road at Raven's Nest.

Go left a few yards towards the house but turn right up a short grassy way to a gate onto the bottom corner of heather-clad Low Moor. Rising away, the splendid green track is quickly joined by a firmer shooters' track, rising with a fence along the edge of the moor. To the left across Raven's Gill are the towers of Yorke's

Folly. 100 yards beyond a gate alongside massive boulders, after a wall takes over, turn left down a slender grassy path. This descends into heather and then bracken to gain the moist environs of Raven's Gill at a ruinous little sheepfold and waterfall. This idyllic spot is best savoured from the grassy bank overlooking the falls.

Across, a thin path slants left out of the gill, fading in heather and bracken on approaching some outcrops. Just behind, a sturdy wall is joined at a boundary stone. Turn right, making use of Open Access to trace a thin wallside path to a gate onto the road on Nought Bank. Drop left to a lay-by, and from the gate behind follow the main path descending the moor. Through a kissing-gate it winds down into Skrikes Wood. A path descends to a stile out of the wood, but remain on the path dropping left through the trees.

The path enjoys a grand descent to Raven's Gill at the bottom. Ignore the footbridge to the left, and turn downstream to leave the wood at a stile. Remain alongside the beck, passing below Skrikes Farm and then slanting up the bank to meet its drive just as it joins a back road. Turn left to a junction, then go left over the bridge to follow a footway back into Bewerley. On the right is Bewerley Grange Chapel. It was built as a grange by Marmaduke Huby, Abbot of Fountains: sympathetically restored in 1965, it stands in peaceful grounds. This is a hugely attractive village with a triangular green and well tended gardens leading to cosy cottages. Continue through the village to complete the walk as you began.

Nought Moor, above Raven's Gill

25

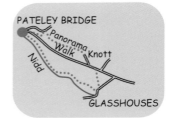

3 miles
from Pateley Bridge

A very simple ramble with views that live up to the name, and a riverside return

Start Town centre (GR: 157655), car parks
Map OS Explorer 298, Nidderdale

From the bridge at the foot of the High Street head up the main thoroughfare, swinging right at the top to quickly level out. After the Methodist Church turn up a flight of steps to the start of the Panorama Walk. A steep, enclosed path climbs past an inscribed stone tablet above a well, with early views up-dale back over the church tower. Beyond the entrance to the cemetery turn left onto a snicket running along to the old church. This offers big views over Bewerley Moor and Gouthwaite Reservoir beyond the gravestones. Hidden in trees in high altitude seclusion, the roofless church of St Mary the Virgin dates from the 14th century: it was abandoned in 1826 due to poor access, insufficient size and repair costs, being replaced by St Cuthbert's church in the town.

Resume by following the path up the churchyard a few yards to locate a wooden kissing-gate in the wall on the right. A nice path crosses a field to a gate, and on again to a stile at the end. A few enclosed yards lead back onto the Panorama Walk. Back on the main route the gradient eases and the narrow surfaced lane continues, enabling views to be appreciated effortlessly. Almost at once an iron gate admits to a viewing platform on a craggy knoll. The Panorama Walk is, not surprisingly, a popular local promenade, and though most Nidderdale walks offer extensive views, none are as easily accessible. Probably the finest feature is the prospect of Guise Cliff directly across the dale, with Yorke's Folly silhouetted.

Reaching the tidy hamlet of Knott, the way widens to drop down to the main road. During this there are good views left to Brimham Rocks, with Summerbridge down-dale amidst rich natural woodland.

Two minutes along the footway to the left, cross to a kissing-gate just past a lone dwelling. A flagged path leads down to a second field, and down to a rough lane on the edge of Glasshouses. Turn left a short way, then past an attractive terrace a very steep, flagged snicket provides a short-cut towards the river. The village is set around a sloping green, with the church spire dominant: its existence owes much to the Metcalfe family, who erected housing and public buildings for workers in their flax spinning mill. Rejoining the road, continue down past the old station and school to approach Glasshouses Bridge. On the left is the mill, dating from 1874 and boasting an imposing facade with old clock and large bell. Today it serves myriad operations and has an impressive riverside frontage.

Without crossing the bridge take the broad carriageway upstream for an infallible return to Pateley Bridge. At once the drive is sandwiched between mill-cut and large millpond, a haven for bird-life. The river is regained at a weir. Across it is the big house of Castlestead, erected in 1862 for the Metcalfes. The Nidd is now traced upstream on an all-weather path. The course of the railway is also in evidence during the final attractive stages, as path and river run together to re-enter town alongside a car park.

Pateley Bridge

*3³⁴ miles
from Pateley Bridge*

**Riverbank walking to visit
a remarkable waterwheel
and sweeping views on
a gentle upland return**

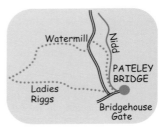

Start **Town centre (GR: 157655), car parks**
Map **OS Explorer 298, Nidderdale**

Pateley Bridge is undisputed capital of Nidderdale: to locals it is the hub of dale life, to visitors, the first stop. Within this compact little town (a village in size) are pubs and cafes, an information centre, a riverside park, with individual and absorbing shops hidden down inviting alleys. The Nidderdale Museum carries absorbing displays of local life gone by, including Pateley Bridge's abandoned industries of lead mining, quarrying and railways. This is also home to the colourful and hugely popular Nidderdale Show each September.

From the foot of the High Street, cross the bridge and turn right into the public park. Remaining on the tree-lined riverbank, the embanked, initially surfaced path leads past a caravan site before gaining open fields. In the second of these the path cuts the corner at Foster Beck's entry into the Nidd, to a kissing-gate to the right of Brigg House Farm. Alongside a cottage a small footbridge crosses the beck, now followed upstream to another kissing-gate before crossing on to a road junction at Corn Close. Turn left, briefly, along the road to the Bridge Inn. This conversion to a pub has replaced the neighbouring Watermill Inn. The original pub had occupied the flax mill that operated as a ropemakers into the 1960s, and restoration of the waterwheel in 1990 made it an attraction in its own right. With the building transformed into apartments, the 35-foot diameter wheel is well seen from the car park.

Continue a little further along the road to a sharp bend, and turn along a stony drive to Mosscarr Farm (a bungalow), ignoring an uphill fork en route as the track opens out to run more pleasantly. Continuing behind barns which cluster island-like in the centre of the field, the track runs on to an idyllically sited cottage at Mosscarr Bottom, bearing a datestone of 1840. Just beyond is a footbridge and ford in a wooded dell. Don't cross, however, but take a kissing-gate to the left. Here a superb grassy way forms, rising left with the wall through increasingly colourful country with unfolding views. At the top corner it passes through a gate and rises to join a firmer track. Just 30 yards further however, with a gate in sight ahead, the right of way bears faintly right, crossing the pasture to find a kissing-gate in the fence ahead, here joining a surfaced access road.

Turn left on this narrow lane rising onto Ladies Riggs, a lofty brow with outstanding views both up-dale and down. About five minutes beyond Riggs House Farm the road enters a shroud of trees: here leave it through the few trees on the left to a stile in a corner. A grand stride follows the hedge downhill with Pateley Bridge ahead. Keeping field boundaries on the right, the way ultimately becomes enclosed to drop down onto a back road at Bridgehouse Gate. Just in front is the splendidly preserved former Metcalf's Brewery, which retains its typical small brewhouse appearance. Go right to the main road by the Royal Oak, then left back over the bridge into town.

Foster Beck Watermill

*4 miles
from Pateley Bridge*

**Absorbing rambling by old
tramway and old railway,
with a lovely old village
and stunning views too**

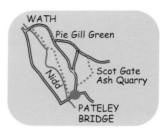

Start Town centre (GR: 157655), car parks
Map OS Explorer 298, Nidderdale

From the bridge head up the High Street and turn left on Church Street, passing the playhouse (1859), Oddfellows Hall and the courthouse (1897). Past St Cuthbert's church continue on Wath Road. After the last row of houses on the left it crosses a bridge, the course of a tramway that served Scot Gate Ash Quarry high above. A stile gives access to the grassy incline whose steep, unremitting course leads unfailingly to the old workings: pauses to savour the view back over town are recommended! The upper stage becomes open and steeper alongside a wood, and from a stile at the top, only a minute's more climbing awaits, and you're there.

These extensive workings produced delphstone, a strong form of millstone grit used as platforms and steps of public buildings. The tramway was operated by steel ropes, with the loaded trucks descending a maximum 1 in 3 gradient as they assisted empty ones return to the top. The descent of 600 feet over a distance of 1000 yards ended at a railway yard at the foot, where it was transferred to a standard gauge line for its journey out of the valley.

With the remains of the winding house ahead, a track heads left, keeping close company with fence or wall. This superb path skirts the lower boundary of the quarry's heathery environs to emerge at the far end. This stunning moment brings sweeping views over the valley, with Great Whernside, Little Whernside and Middlesmoor beyond Gouthwaite Reservoir. Head on through a gateway to cross to a gate onto Wath Lane. This quiet byway leads all the way back to the valley, an extended descent in which you can concentrate exclusively on the panorama, major feature being the penetration of the upper dale by Gouthwaite Reservoir.

At a junction continue ahead, down to another junction at Pie Gill Green. Turn right for a couple of minutes into Wath. This tiny, unspoiled settlement boasts a fine wooded setting with much of interest. First is the tiny Methodist chapel of 1859 affixed to a cottage. At the bend beyond is an old mill with bell, weathervane and workers' cottages. The Sportsmans Arms has a fine individual sign, while across from it is the old station house. Remain on the road as it turns sharp left past the hotel, over the old railway and along to Wath Bridge. Though widened in 1890 it is small enough to recall the days when it served the monks of Fountains Abbey.

Without crossing the bridge take a footbridge on the left: a path crosses a field centre to a wall-stile, continuing on to meet the slightly embanked course of the old railway. From the next stile the line is followed for some distance to a point where the Nidd comes in alongside. Beyond a stile in this tree-shrouded setting the railway is forsaken for the river, whose tree-lined bank leads unerringly back to Pateley Bridge. Part way along, note the lively confluence at the arrival of Foster Beck. Reaching a weir the path becomes confined, and is deflected away to emerge between buildings onto Mill Lane adjacent to Pateley's graceful bridge.

Wath Bridge

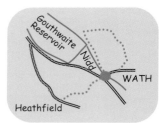

*3¹2 miles
from Wath*

**Steady rambling looks
down on both sides of
Nidderdale's most
scenic sheet of water**

*Start Village centre (GR: 145677), parking at Wath Bridge
Map OS Explorer 298, Nidderdale*

Wath is a tiny, unspoiled settlement in a fine wooded setting. The Sportsmans Arms features an individual sign, while a tiny Methodist chapel affixed to a cottage dates from 1859. Head east from the hotel to the old mill, with its bell, weathervane, and workers' cottages. As the road turns sharp right just past here, leave by an access road left past a mullioned windowed cottage. The track climbs through woodland to a fork. Keep left on past an old farm at Spring Wood Top. Immediately past is a deep quarry hole filled with water. The track then makes a gentle descent with Gouthwaite Reservoir coming more into view.

You pass directly above the masonry dam, and a couple of fields later, leave the track by a gate on the left. This is a good spot to look over the extensive lake, built in 1909 as a compensation reservoir for the large watermills downstream, and today highly valued for its bird-life. The 80-foot high dam is camouflaged by foliage and sets the scene for this least intrusive of Nidderdale's reservoirs. A mostly naturally wooded shoreline masks the harshness of man's hand: indeed, it could be argued this is merely a return to colder times, when a glacial lake filled the dale floor.

A part-kerbed green track doubles back down the field to the very edge of the dam wall. Here you encounter the grassy course of the Nidd Valley Light Railway. From a small gate by the dam end, the path drops through trees to emerge into a pasture alongside the Nidd. Cross to a stile and then the last long pasture is a charming riverside stroll to a stile onto the road at Wath Bridge. Embowered in greenery, this lovely arched structure was originally a packhorse bridge. though widened in 1890, it is small enough to recall the days when it served the monks of Fountains Abbey. Cross the bridge and head north along the road, passing the reservoir dam and tracing the wooded shoreline for a near half-mile until a narrow, winding strip of tarmac doubles sharply back through a cattle-grid on the left. Unsigned and resembling a private drive, this traffic-free lane rises steeply, affording extensive views back over the reservoir and further updale.

Passing through the dense West Wood, the road levels out at the scattered group of dwellings at Heathfield. This ancient settlement had a fulling mill under the auspices of the monks of Byland Abbey, while the ubiquitous Yorke family smelted ore here from their lead mines. A corrugated green shack on the roadside is the old Methodist chapel. As the lane slowly descends, opt for the drive left down to Spring Hill Farm. The path skirts the right hand exterior of the yard and winds round to a stile at the far end of the field. From it descend half-left through two large fields, then straight over two smaller ones to drop steeply back to the road at Wath Bridge, with the centre just a minute further along the lane.

Gouthwaite Reservoir from above Wath

33

*4 miles
from Ramsgill*

**A very uncomplicated
linear walk to
the high moors
overlooking Ramsgill**

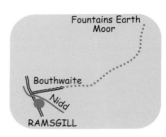

Start Village centre (GR: 119709), roadside parking
without impinging on green, reserved for hotel patrons
Map OS Explorer 298, Nidderdale (or OL30)

Ramsgill is the showpiece village of the upper dale, on the banks of its own beck just short of its confluence with the Nidd. At the heart is a spacious green, where attractive cottages and flowery gardens play support to the imposing ivy-clad hotel. The Yorke Arms is a former shooting lodge still bearing the name of its one-time occupants. A circular stone pinfold stands in front of the village hall. The church of St Mary the Virgin looks out across the reedy head of Gouthwaite Reservoir. Ramsgill was an important grange of Byland Abbey, and a solitary gable-end at the rear of the church remains from the monks' chapel.

From the green head north past the hotel on the Lofthouse road, but immediately after crossing Nidd Bridge turn right on the narrow lane to Bouthwaite. En route, the course of the Nidd Valley Light Railway is crossed, adjacent to the old station house. The railway opened in 1908 to convey material and men for construction of the Angram dam at the dalehead. It also operated as a passenger line, but completion of Scar House dam in 1936 saw the end of its useful life. Passing a former Wesleyan chapel of 1890, the road ends at a junction of tracks in the centre of the hamlet. Note a still working, locally manufactured clock on the out-building on your left. Less than ten miles distant from this point, Fountains Abbey had an important grange here.

Go straight ahead to a gate, beyond which a stony track sets about scaling the hillside. Suitable halts earn wide views back over the dale, including to Gouthwaite Reservoir, while beyond Ramsgill the side valley of Ramsgill Beck tumbles from the moors. When the gradient eases the going underfoot improves, rising all the way to Intake Gate and a junction at a wall corner. The track continuing uphill is the old road to Kirkby Malzeard via Dallowgill. These once important highways that linked Upper Nidderdale with its monastic landlords today serve only walkers, shooting parties and the occasional off-road biker.

Branch left for a near level stroll to a second fork at a choice of gates. This is of little consequence as this is pretty much the end of your wanderings. In front, far ahead, the rock outcrops of Sypeland Crags break the skyline across the heather of Fountains Earth Moor. The moor is named, unsurprisingly, from its former monastic owners. All that remains is the pleasurable task of retracing steps back down to Bouthwaite and thence Ramsgill.

Ramsgill from above Bouthwaite

4¹2 miles
from Lofthouse Moor

**Largely level walking
entirely on the
high moors: save it
for a clear day**

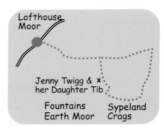

Start Pott Moor High Road at top of climb on Masham road
out of Lofthouse (GR: 113749), roadside parking on a bend
where the road bridges Backstone Gill
Map OS Explorer 298, Nidderdale
Access Open Access land from the shooting house over
Sypeland Crags, no dogs allowed: can be closed on a
limited number of days, see contact details on page 5

Ignoring the bridleway that heads off through a gate
from the bend, instead head along the road (away from Lofthouse)
for just a minute and then bear right along a rougher surfaced
road. Here stands an illegible old milestone. The walled lane runs to
a gate onto Longside Moor, then continues as a wallside track to
quickly arrive at a fork. Bear left, running open and rising slightly
to the next gate. Again a wall provides some company, soon passing
a stone shooting cabin from where the intriguing boulders of Jenny
Twigg and her Daughter Tib are seen through the gate. Assuming
access land is open (and you've no dog), then through the gate a
grassy shooters' track heads down past a line of butts, from where
cross to quickly gain the stones. This giant pair are splendid landmarks, young Tib being little short of her mother in stature.

Continue contouring left past a number of other lone
outcrops, including a particularly shapely bridestone. Just behind is
a wall-cum-fence. Cross at the hurdle junction and go right to the
steep edge, the start of Sypeland Crags. Now simply follow this

broken edge all the way along, either above or below, encountering a host of spectacularly shaped gritstone boulders. As they end, contour round a little further and then drop down to cross Lul Beck to join another firm old track just above. Turn left up this, rising gently through the heather of Fountains Earth Moor, named from its former monastic owners. After passing through a gate a small inscribed boundary stone is passed, as you continue rising to arrive at a major junction alongside another boundary stone.

By now you have a massive sweeping vista over the Kirkby Malzeard moors to the Vale of Mowbray, backed by Teesside and the North York Moors, featuring Roseberry Topping, the Cleveland Hills and the Hambleton Hills, and also the Yorkshire Wolds. The continuing track is the old road that engages several more upland miles towards Kirkby Malzeard and Masham. Your route, however, doubles back left to run on to rejoin the outward route alongside the shooting house, and retrace opening steps back to the start.

Jenny Twigg and her Daughter Tib

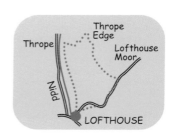

*3¼ miles
from Lofthouse*

**A steep climb
is rewarded with
outstanding views over
Upper Nidderdale**

*Start Village centre (GR: 101735), car park
Map OS Explorer 298, Nidderdale (or OL30)*

Lofthouse is a tidy village high above the river, featuring the Crown Hotel and an attractive corner which includes the Post office and a water fountain which bears words worth reading. A house opposite the memorial institute bears a 1653 datestone. Alongside the school and WC on the bottom road is the old station house, the highest on the Nidd Valley Light Railway. Leave by the Masham road which passes the Peace Memorial before climbing away from the houses, but before the first bend leave it by a grassy track left. This is Thrope Lane, and beyond a gate it leads an unerring, mile-long course to Thrope Farm. Already you have good views across to Middlesmoor from this splendid old track. There is a brief glimpse to your objective of the shooting house on Thrope Edge, appearing as a church silhouetted on the skyline. The track becomes enclosed for the final section to the farm.

As you draw level with the farm take a gate on the right to negotiate sheep pens, past a barn and up the wallside. Towards the top bear left to a gate in the fence above. Entering more colourful surrounds rise left with the fence, an old green way soon forking. Ignoring its sunken continuation, instead bear right up a similarly good track. This ascends steeply through scattered silver birch and bracken, then swings left to rise more steadily above the trees and beneath scattered rocks. Outstanding views now open out over the upper dale, featuring the mid-height shelf of The

Edge as the valley curves round towards its bleak head. This finely engineered old track slants all the way up to a gate in the wall above, and through it the shooting house is revealed just a little higher. Crossing the few reeds on your left, a continuing grassy way rises to gain the skyline of Thrope Edge just left of the house.

This is emphatically the place to halt and embrace the big views along the length of the dale. A fine contrast is formed by the lush green of the valley at your feet and the dark outlines of rounded Meugher, Great Whernside and Little Whernside on the western skyline, with Menwith Hill and Greenhow Hill way down the valley. Turn right on the broad shooters' track alongside, enjoying only a short spell above the edge before a wall deflects the track left. Within a minute take a gate in the wall and a nicer grassier track heads away across the moor. As a wall comes in on the left continue above a recolonised quarry, and as the fading track forks bear left to a gateway in the wall. Gouthwaite Reservoir makes its big appearance straight ahead. The track gently declines through two moorland enclosures to a gate onto Pott Moor High Road.

Turn right to commence a short, steep descent back to Lofthouse, with views featuring Gouthwaite, the Stean Valley and Middlesmoor. When the road breaks free turn down the wallside for a more direct, grassy descent to the edge of the village.

Thrope Lane

*2¾ miles
from Lofthouse*

**Varied natural attractions
either side of the
centrepiece attraction
of Upper Nidderdale**

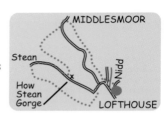

*Start Village centre (GR: 101735), car park
Map OS Explorer 298, Nidderdale (or OL30)*

From the fountain take a gap in the corner of the square between cottages, and a path runs down a fieldside to a footbridge on the Nidd. Upstream are the lovely Nidd Falls. Cross to emerge onto the Scar House road, straight over to a kissing-gate and past a cricket pitch to a kissing-gate onto a road. Go briefly right then fork left on the How Stean Gorge branch. Past a car park it bridges How Stean Beck. Cross and turn left to Studfold Farm. Turn sharp right up the steep, rough road to some cottages. Continue, ignoring a branch left before levelling out. After a renovated farmhouse take a gate on the right, and a grassy track crosses field bottoms to Whitbeck Farm. En route enjoy super views over Lofthouse to Thrope Edge, with Middlesmoor across the How Stean valley.

A slim stile to the right accesses the drive, then go left up into the yard. Turn right through a gate to drop to a footbridge, then resume on field bottoms (via wall-stiles) to the next farm. A few yards of flagged path lead to a small gate into its confines. Go straight ahead between house and barns, and out via a gap-stile into a field. Cross to another just ahead, then continue between a tiny stream and wall to the bottom corner, where a single slab bridge crosses a tiny beck to enter an attractive corner of the farming hamlet of Stean. Turn downhill to leave by the access road.

The road runs quickly along to the entrance to How Stean Gorge. En route you pass good views into the ravine to whet your appetite. If opting to explore the gorge, pay entrance fees at the cafe/gift shop. How Stean Gorge is a limestone ravine half a mile long and up to 80 feet deep, its rocks worn into dramatic contours by the action of the swift-flowing water: deep, dark and wet caves abound. The expedition is but a short one, downstream of the cafe being especially exciting as the path negotiates dramatically suspended bridges to guarded natural walkways through the rocks.

Resume across the bridge to the car park field and take a gate at the top left corner. Advance to a gate by a barn, then go left across several field-centres, using gates in walls beneath Hazel Close Farm to meet a path from Middlesmoor at a wall-stile. Don't pass through but turn up to a stile above, and ascend two fieldsides to emerge onto a road just beneath the entrance to Middlesmoor. Ascend into the village past an old Wesleyan chapel of 1899, with the Crown pub in an attractive corner just above.

Leave by making for the church by a cobbled street after the phone box. To its right a squeezer-stile sees a short snicket down to a gate. A flight of steps drops into a field, and a path maintains a straight line to Halfway House Farm. Go straight through the yard to a gate at the bottom, and head down the right side of a field to a stile. At the bottom swing left to a stile part way along, then bear left to a corner stile to emerge onto the lay-by near the start of the walk. Retrace steps over the footbridge, but consider a five-minute detour upstream for the shy charms of Nidd Falls.

Nidd Falls, Lofthouse

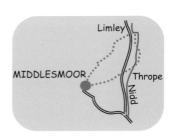

*3 miles
from Middlesmoor*

**A leisurely dip into
the upper dale
from its characterful
highest village**

Start Village centre (GR: 092742), car park at top end
Map OS Explorer 298, Nidderdale (or OL30)

Middlesmoor's name reflects its position on a broad
tongue between the valley of the Nidd and its tributary How Stean
Beck. The Crown Inn occupies a very attractive corner across from
the old school: an old tablet informs of its building in 1807. An
intricate network of alleyways wind between gritstone cottages
with flowery gardens to the church, visited at the end of the walk.
Leave by a small gate at the start of a farmyard immediately
beneath the car park. A little path crosses the field to pass along
the top of a slender wood, emerging to cross to a wall-stile ahead.
Gouthwaite Reservoir is well seen down-dale. Advance on above the
farm at Smithfield Hall to the next stile, then on to one to your
left to join the access road approaching Northside Head Farm.

Pass round to the left after which a mercurial grassy
track takes over, running on through several gates with superb
views over the upper dale. Your goal Limley Farm is in the bottom,
with Dale Edge and Thrope Edge on the skyline. On becoming
enclosed at the start of How Gill Plantation, take a stile/gate on
the right and a thin path descends the field, slanting left over a
tiny stream to a wall-stile in the very corner. Slant again to a small
gateway near the corner below, with a wall-stile just beneath. Now
slant down to one below, and down one last field to a stile onto the
Scar House road. Cross straight over to another, and along to a
gate by barns and then a stile into Limley Farm.

Turn right on the drive out, but as it swings up to the road go left to a gate. Bear left to a path dropping with a fence to a stile into the wooded confines of the dry Nidd (which disappeared a short way upstream). A path runs past a stone-arched level, soon crossing a stile to resume downstream to a gate accessing Dry Wath, a suitable name for the ford you use to cross the stony riverbed. Resume downstream on the fieldside until deflected left by a wall. A part sunken way rises with it to a gate, and the grassy track runs on to approach Thrope Farm. Enclosed for the final yards to a gate, turn down through the yard and down the drive to cross the river.

Cross the fence to head down the bank, but approaching a wall bear right through a gateway. Slant to a stile near the far corner, and a few strides left on the Scar House road to another one. From a wall-stile behind rise to a fine one above, then cross a large field to the next ascending wall, and up to a gate at the top. Don't pass through but go left with the wall to pass through a slim wood. Ascend a large field to a fence-stile above, with some of Middlesmoor's houses just above. Above this is a gate, through which curve up to a gate in the corner just above to re-enter the village near the church. St Chad's is an attractive church on an ancient foundation: a Saxon cross within is said to have been Chad's 7th century preaching cross. It is perhaps better known as a view-point, with the churchyard as foreground to a renowned panorama down the length of the dale, to Gouthwaite Reservoir and beyond.

The Crown, Middlesmoor

*3½ miles
from Limley*

**A splendid exploration of
the upper dale, with big
views, famous potholes
and an elusive river**

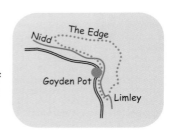

Start Roadside parking area (GR: 099764), alongside old
rail tunnel entrance a half-mile north of Limley Farm
Map OS Explorer 298, Nidderdale (or OL30)

Opposite the parking area a short path drops through
scrub to a stile. Facing you at the field bottom is Manchester Hole,
under the cliff of Beggarmoat Scar. The River Nidd might quietly
depart underground here - or not. Trace the fence downstream on
the field edge, over a brow and down to a gate. Just beyond, the
dark hole of Goyden Pot sits in a crook of the riverbed. When the
flow of water is sufficiently strong, the excess from Manchester
Hole is carried to this point. The 'real' Nidd then enjoys two sub-
terranean miles, re-emerging below Lofthouse. While the main
chamber can be entered when dry, the inner depths contain a maze
of passages emphatically only suitable for experienced cavers.

Resume down the grassy bank above limestone outcrops,
crossing Limley Gill and quickly becoming an enclosed grassy way to
reach Limley Farm. This attractive grouping is the site of a grange
of Byland Abbey. Enter the yard by a gate right of a house, going
first right then left to pass round the buildings. Behind the last
barn a path descends to cross the riverbed to a gate. Beyond it
carry on by an old wall. Before a barn, fork right up an inviting
branch path. Here begins the only uphill of the walk. With a few
stone steps in place, this zigzags up the steep bank, turning left at
the top to meet another grassy zigzag. The upper part runs to a
gate to reach Thwaite House, site of a grange of Fountains Abbey.

From a gate left of the buildings head off on the access road, a splendid, enclosed cart track that soon emerges into open country. You are now treated to spacious views over this great curve of the upper dale; the tree-lined river winds below, while the dam of Scar House appears under Little Whernside. Reaching Bracken Ridge there is no need to enter the yard. Note, however, the lovely old barn at the top side, with mullioned windows and a 1626 datestone. Turn up onto the access road heading away to begin a lengthy traverse of The Edge. This broad track is a fine platform along which several farms and cottages are based, taking advantage of a spring line occasionally in evidence. Looking ahead, Little Whernside is joined by the shoulder of Great Whernside.

With a wall to the left and steep slopes right, the track runs pleasurably on to New Houses Edge Farm, last settlement on The Edge. Approaching here, Great Whernside's summit slots into place at the dalehead. Beyond the farm the track fords a stream to enter open pasture. Just a little further it forks: take the left branch, descending. Reaching a gate near a barn, the track crosses fields to approach the river, which it follows downstream to New Houses Bridge. Don't cross but go straight ahead to a gate near the river, and along the bank to a stile to continue downstream to avoid New Houses Farm. Follow the Nidd downstream a couple of fields before trading banks at a footbridge. After a pair of neighbouring stiles, Manchester Hole is reached, with the start just up the bank.

Little Whernside and Upper Nidderdale from above Goyden Pot

*4 miles
from Scar House*

**A simple circuit of this
windswept reservoir in
its bleak upland setting**

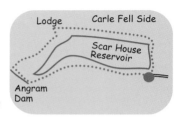

Start Water company car park at road end, accessed
from the Middlesmoor road near Lofthouse (GR: 068766)
Map OS Explorer 298, Nidderdale (small section on
OL30, Yorkshire Dales North/Central, but not essential)

From the car park join the water company road which
runs past the dam of Scar House Reservoir - not crossed until the
end of the walk. The road, meanwhile, runs along the entire length
of the southern shore. There is a regular supply of benches to rest
on, even though you shouldn't exactly need a rest! At the dalehead,
the rippling shoulders of Great Whernside form a comprehensive
barrier: over to the right is flat-topped Little Whernside.

The road eventually gains the foot of Angram Reservoir,
not seen until you are almost there. Just short of it stands a rest
house, a quaint facility provided by the water company, certainly
appreciated if caught by a sudden shower. Identical in character
(though Scar House is double the size) Angram was completed in
1913, 23 years before its lower neighbour. Both the handiwork of
Bradford Corporation, each boasts a masonry dam of which Scar
House's rises to a height of some 150 feet. Beneath Angram's
chilly waters is a farm that was once the highest in the dale, on the
site of a small grange of Byland Abbey.

Head across the dam to its northern end, and then turn
right onto an excellent green path, running gently downstream and
soon swinging left to begin a contour that is interrupted only by the
little dip of Wench Gill. Good views look down over Scar House
Reservoir to Carle Fell and Dale Edge. Rising back out to a gate, the

path resumes, soon joined by a wall to reach a gate in a fence. Just beyond, a gate admits to the terminus of an enclosed green way.

An option here is to return by the waterside path, in which case pass through a stile on the right and descend the wall-side to the shore. Go left through a gate to another rest house, then simply trace an excellent path all the way back to the end of the dam. The main route turns left up the enclosed track which swings right to a junction. Turn right here to at once reach the Lodge. Only scant ruins survive from what was originally a medieval hunting lodge, and a working farm until a century ago. Embowered in trees, this location is prominent in all views around this dalehead.

This same track now leads high above Scar House Reservoir's northern shore. Enjoy big views beyond the dam to the magnificent sweep of the upper valley beneath the moors of Dale Edge. Across the valley below the car park can be seen the site of a village that existed during the construction years: this complete settlement had little short of 100 children schooled here in the 1920s. On the hillsides, meanwhile, are the sites of quarries opened to win stone for the dams. Everything was on site, including, no doubt, very soon the water! Another rest house is reached above the dam, with Scar House itself just ahead. Now cross the dam to return to the car park, and take a look back across the dam wall to the extensive Carle Fell Quarry you have just passed beneath.

Scar House Reservoir

HILLSIDE GUIDES... cover much of Northern England

Other colour *Pocket Walks* guides (available during 2009)
·UPPER WHARFEDALE ·MALHAMDALE ·NIDDERDALE
·LOWER WHARFEDALE ·AIRE VALLEY ·HARROGATE
·AMBLESIDE & LANGDALE ·BORROWDALE ·BOWLAND

Our *Walking Country* range features more great walks...

·WHARFEDALE   ·MALHAMDALE   ·WENSLEYDALE
·HARROGATE & the WHARFE VALLEY ·SWALEDALE
·RIPON & LOWER WENSLEYDALE   ·NIDDERDALE
·THREE PEAKS   ·HOWGILL FELLS
·TEESDALE   ·EDEN VALLEY   ·ALSTON & ALLENDALE

·NORTH YORK MOORS, SOUTH   ·HOWARDIAN HILLS

·ILKLEY MOOR ·BRONTE COUNTRY   ·CALDERDALE
·PENDLE & the RIBBLE   ·WEST PENNINE MOORS
·ARNSIDE & SILVERDALE   ·LUNESDALE   ·BOWLAND

·LAKELAND FELLS, SOUTH   ·LAKELAND FELLS, EAST
·LAKELAND FELLS, NORTH   ·LAKELAND FELLS, WEST

Long Distance Walks, including
·COAST TO COAST WALK ·CUMBRIA WAY ·DALES WAY
·LADY ANNE'S WAY ·BRONTE WAY ·NIDDERDALE WAY
·WESTMORLAND WAY   ·FURNESS WAY   ·PENDLE WAY

Also available
·YORKSHIRE DALES, MOORS & FELLS
·THE HIGH PEAKS OF ENGLAND & WALES

Visit www.hillsidepublications.co.uk
or write for a catalogue